the art of argument

an introduction to the informal fallacies

TEACHER'S MATERIALS

by aaron larsen

and joelle hodge

The Art of Argument
© Classical Academic Press, 2003-2007
Version 7.0

ISBN: 1-60051-019-1
EAN: 9781600510199

Classical Academic Press
3920 Market Street
Camp Hill, PA 17011

www.classicalacademicpress.com

TEACHER'S MATERIALS

Introduction

This book of teacher's materials contains three sections:

1) A key containing answers for the student text
2) A section of additional quizzes and tests not included in the student text
3) A key for all these additional quizzes and tests

Here are some comments and suggestions pertaining to each section:

Answer Key for the student edition of *The Art of Argument*
This key should be used by teachers in order to assess a student's answers to the various exercises in the text. Please note that not every section in the student book that requires a student response contains a corresponding answer in the key. For example, those sections in the student text named "Further Research" and "Application" do not always have answers in the key. This is because some of these questions may involve a student's personal opinion or may direct him to find examples of fallacies in the general media. However, whenever we thought that something helpful could be recorded in the key we have done so.

Additional Quizzes and Tests
Teachers may want to give students additional tests beyond those contained in the student text. We have created this section for this purpose. The quizzes and tests in this section may also be used as additional exercises when more practice defining or identifying fallacies is needed.

Answer Key for Quizzes and Tests
This section contains answers for all the quizzes and tests in the previous section. Students can check their own work using this key or teachers can use the key to grade the quizzes and tests.

. . . .

Review Exercises
Lesson 1.1: What is Logic? Fight Fair!

Vocabulary: Define each of the following terms.

1. What are the positive and negative senses of the word "argument?"
Positive: When people engage in discussion and debate without personal attack, bickering or quarreling in order to discover, clarify and more fully understand what is true, correct or wise.
Negative: When people engage in discussion and debate while also bickering, quarreling and personally attacking each other, with little regard to actually discover, clarify and more fully understand what is true, correct or wise.

2. How do arguments sometimes violate the principle of relevance?

Oftentimes people make arguments that are simply not relevant to the issue at hand. Whenever someone argues for something, or introduces facts, issues, testimonies and evidence that do not truly bear on the issue at hand, he or she is violating the principle of relevance.

3. How do arguments sometimes violate the principle of presumption?

Whenever people assume (or presume) something that is illegitimate in the course of making an argument they violate the principle of presumption. Usually people make these assumptions in a stealthy, hidden manner that is hard to detect.

4. How do arguments sometimes violate the principle of clarity?

Whenever people making arguments use language in a way that is confusing, tricky or deceiving they are violating the principle of clarity.

. . . .

Review Exercises
Lesson 1.2: Critical Thinking as a Way of Life

A. Vocabulary: Define each of the following terms. Include their etymology.
1. **Philosopher**: The etymology literally means a "lover of wisdom." In a more technical and contemporary sense it means a student of philosophy.
2. **philos:** Greek for "loving"
3. **sophia:** Greek for "wisdom"
4. **Metaphysics:** The branch of academic philosophy that deals with the question "What is really real?"
5. **Epistemology:** The branch of academic philosophy that deals with the question "How can we know what we know?"
6. **Socrates:** The Mentor of Plato who is considered by many to be the founder of Western philosophy.

B. Further research:

Write a short essay answering both of the following questions. Use available classroom resources, internet sites, or library resources.

1. Why do you think the authors of the text consider Socrates to be "perhaps the greatest example" of a philosopher?

   The essay should include points like the following:
   a. Socrates is great in the sense of being famous and well-known, even outside

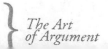

of those who study philosophy. He was one of the first philosophers (he was born around 470 B.C.).

b. Socrates is great in the sense that he has had a great influence. His student Plato (also a famous philosopher) recorded many of Socrates teaching in the form of dialogues. These dialogues have a great, enduring influence in the history of philosophy and literature.

c. Socrates is great in the sense that he personified the quintessential "lover of wisdom." He constantly asked questions of himself and others in order to discover wisdom.

2. Discuss the importance of a class in logic. The authors suggest I Peter 3:15 for our consideration. What example do we have as Christians to be prepared and successfully argue for our faith rather than arguing like a demagogue?

This essay should include points like the following:
a. A class in informal logic will help students to protect themselves against faulty, deceptive arguments.
b. A class in informal logic will help students to craft arguments that are relevant and clear.
c. Christians are exhorted to argue with "gentleness and respect" which follows from the examples of Christ and the apostles. Peter reminds us that our attitude, demeanor and very life are just as important (perhaps more) than any argument we craft in words.

. . . .

Review Exercise
Lesson 1.3: Formal vs. Informal Logic

A. Etymology and Vocabulary: Define each of the following terms. Include their etymology.

1. **Logic:** The art and science of reasoning. Logos = Greek for "reason."
2. **Formal Logic:** The branch of logic that deals with the form or structure of argument and emphasizes deductive reasoning. *Forma* is Latin for "form" or "shape." *In + forma* = lacking form or shape.
3. **Informal Logic:** The branch of logic that deals with the guidelines for sound reasoning in ordinary-language arguments
4. **Deductive Reasoning:** Reasoning that involves arguments that have a form or structure such that if the premises are given, the conclusion must follow. *Deduco* is Latin for "I lead down."
5. **Inductive Reasoning:** Reasoning that involves arguments built from the evidence of the senses and in which the conclusions only follow with more or less probability. *Induco* is Latin for "I lead in."

K

B. Further research:

Write a short essay answering the following questions. Use available classroom resources, internet sites, or library resources.

1. How does C.L. Hamblin characterize the differences between the two kinds of reasoning? Who is C.L. Hamblin? [hint: see footnote for ideas.]

2. Which type of reasoning do you think is most important? Why?

. . . .

Review Exercises
Dialogue 1.4: On Logic . . . and Propaganda

A. Etymology and Vocabulary: Define each of the following terms. Include their etymology.
1. **Fallacy:** A bad argument that follows one of several patterns recognized by students of logic. **Fallacia** is Latin for "deceit," "trick," and "fraud."
2. **Relevant:** Having to do with the main issue, rather than a distracting side issue. **Relevare** is Latin for "to raise up."
3. **Persuasion:** The art of convincing others. **Persuadere** is Latin for "to persuade."
4. **Propaganda:** Persuasive techniques targeting large numbers of people. **Propagare** is Latin for "to spread, propagate, extend."

B. Further Research:
Write a short essay answering each of the following questions. Use available classroom resources, internet sites, newspapers or magazines.
1. How would you define the Principle of Relevance? Use available classroom resources, internet sites, newspapers or magazines.

> **Principle of Relevance: The principle that requires a person making an argument to relate that argument to the issue at hand and not stray from the issue by introducing evidence and arguments, that no-matter how compelling, are not relevant to the issue at hand.**

2. Find three examples of Non-Argumentative Persuasion from newspapers, magazines or a book.

3. Fine three examples of the Appeal to Illegitimate Authority from newspapers, magazines or a book.. (Also give the name of this fallacy in Latin). **Argumentum ad Verecundiam**

The Art

Review Exercises
Chapter 3.7: Ad Fontem Argument Worksheet

A. Define: In cases of Latin terms, also give the translation:

1. ***Ad Fontem Arguments:*** Arguments directed at the source. Translation: "to the source or fountain."

2. ***Ad Hominem Abusive:*** Arguments that distract from the source by hurling abuse at a rival speaker. Translation: "to the man."

3. ***Ad Hominem Circumstantial:*** Arguments that distract from the main issue by pointing to the circumstances of a rival speaker. Translation: "to the man."

4. ***Tu Quoque:*** Arguments that distract from the main issue by pointing out that the rival speaker has not always been consistent with his current position. Translation: "you also."

5. **Genetic Fallacy:** Arguments that distract from the main issue by pointing to the (impersonal) source of the argument.

B. Identification:

Which Ad Fontem Argument is being described below? Explain your answer by telling why it can't be one of the other "Ad Fontem Arguments". (Hint: the "Key Points" might be helpful.)

1. An argument directed against the circumstances of the speaker's rival.
   ad hominem circumstantial

2. An argument involving obviously abusive language.
   ad hominem abusive

3. An argument centered entirely on the inconsistencies exhibited by the speaker's rival.
   tu quoque

4. An argument that isn't directed as a person; an impersonal attack.
   genetic fallacy

C. Applicaiton:

Find or write 2 examples of the *Ad Fontem Argument*. You may use internet sites, books, newspapers or magazines.

The Art

CUMULATIVE FALLACY WORKSHEET I

DIRECTIONS: under each example, write both the category and the specific fallacy.

1. It's time to take all of your money out of the stock market. The Y2K thing is going to crash all of the stock markets everywhere and the Asian crisis is going to spread to this country. How do I know? Well, all the experts are predicating a speedy recovery and they were predicting just such a thing before the Great Depression.
   appeal to fear

2. Yesterday on *Fox News Sunday* Britt Hume strongly argued that we should take military action against Iraq. But you can't trust anything on that right-wing news organization.
   genetic fallacy

3. Don't vote for Howard Stern, because he's a long-haired, dope-smoking, maggot-infested FM-type.
   ad hominem abusive

4. If you elect those heartless Republicans to congress, they'll leave all of the poor, under-privileged schoolchildren without a square meal because of all of the cutbacks in school lunch funding that they advocate.
   appeal to pity

5. You shouldn't comment on the abortion issue because you're a man and you couldn't possibly know what an unwed mother goes through.
   ad hominem circumstantial

6. Mr. Jones has no right to tell us to study hard, because he admits that he was a poor student when he was our age.
   tu quoque

7. Vote for Harkin, champion of the working man!
   mob appeal

8. How can that speaker expect us to follow his advice and not use drugs when he admits using them himself in the past?
   tu quoque

The Art
of Argument

Review Exercises
Chapter 4.11: Appeals to Emotion Worksheet

A. Define. Define completely naming each type of the following fallacy. In cases of Latin terms, also give the translation:

1. Appeals to Emotion: Fallacies that very directly target an emotional reaction.

2. Argumentum ad Populum: Fallacies that target a need for "belonging" or for myth of the "common man."

3. Argumentum ad Baculum: Fallacies that target the emotion of fear.

4. Argumentum ad Misericordia: Fallacies that target the emotion of pity.

5. Snob Appeal: Fallacies that target feelings of elitism.

6. Ad Verecundiam: An appeal to authority (which tends to target feelings of humility, or "verecundiam" in the audience.)

7. Chronological Snobbery: Fallacies that assume that the age of something in itself is a reason to accept or reject it.

B. Chronological Snobbery Review:

All of the examples below are cases of chronological snobbery. Identify the examples that emphasize tradition by putting a **"T"** in the blank and those that rely on Novelty by putting an **"N"** in the blank.

___T___ Yuengling Lager; brewed by America's oldest brewery.

___N___ Come down to the Bon-Ton's sale and pick up this summer's latest fashions before they're all gone!

___N___ Don't tell me you're reading H.D.F. Kitto's The Greeks! That book was written a generation ago! You should pick up something that reflects the latest research.

___N___ Don't tell me that you oppose bill # 3129! Mark my words, you cannot oppose the march of Progress.

___T___ We can't change now, we've always done it that way.

K

C. Identification:

Which Appeal to Emotion Argument is being described below? Explain your answer.

Bob suspected his company was involved in some illegal activities. He decided to resign and on his last day, he stole a file containing incriminating evidence from a coworker. He had plans to take the file to a lawyer. The company executives found out about the missing file and sent a message to Bob in a very unconventional way. They leaked the story to a reporter at a local television station, of course omitting the details about the contents of the file.

The next morning, Bob watched the news in amazement as the reporter recounted the details relayed to him by the company. His picture flashed on the screen as the reporter named Bob as the prime suspect in the case.

That afternoon, Bob received a call from one of the executives informing him that the smear campaign would last as long as he was in possession of the file. The executive reminded Bob that was unemployed, and looking for a job. The executive asked him questions about his future. How did he expect to find work if employers suspected him to be a thief, a whistle-blower and a criminal? The executive encouraged Bob to think about his actions and return the file immediately.

(ANSWERS MAY VARY, BUT IT'S CLEARLY AN APPEAL TO FEAR.)

D. Application:

Name all three types of Appeal to Illegitimate Authority. Then, create or find two examples of each.

The following points could be made:

1. The real issue for the advertisers is the objective motivating the reader to buy their product.
2. Their product likely has something to do with cleaning or purifying water.
3. By asking the reader to question the purity of his water the advertisers are appealing to fear—especially by showing an image with the "questionable" water flowing over a person's face!
4. No doubt an advertisement like this may succeed in selling a product, but it is not a successful argument. The mere asking of the question does not establish that one has impure water.

CUMULATIVE FALLACY WORKSHEET II

DIRECTIONS: under each example, write both the category and the specific fallacy.

1. It's foolish to keep a gun in the house for self-defense. I read just the other day that more people are killed in accidents with guns than are killed by people breaking into their houses.
   appeal to fear

2. There are certain people who demand more of their trucks than 99% of all truck owners. We call them the "one-percenter." For them, we make GMC trucks.
   snob appeal

3. The Labor Party proposal must be fought with every ounce of our strength. Such a hoary and respected institution as the House of Lords simply ought not to be tampered with.
   chronological snobbery

4. Buy a Ford truck, transportation for the American working man!
   mob appeal (argumentum ad populum)

5. You can't be serious in believing in a young earth. The vast majority of scientists in this country believe in an old earth.
   mob appeal *in the sense that it is relying on a majority opinion, but it could be snob appeal in the sense that scientists are a sort of elite within society.*

6. The Republicans in Congress would be foolish to impeach Clinton; 63% of the American people oppose it.
   mob appeal

7. You really ought to take Jen to the prom, Jon. Just think of how sad and lonely she'll be if you don't.
   appeal to pity

8. "Hi, I'm Dan Marino, former quarter back for the Miami Dolphins. If you need money, come see the friendly folks at the Money Store."
   appeal to illegitimate authority *(argumentum ad verecundiam)*

9. Senator Helm's argument concerning the tobacco bill ought to be discounted, as he is obviously not objective. The tobacco companies are his biggest campaign contributors.
   ad hominem circumstantial

Review Exercises
Chapter 5.6: Red Herrings:

A. Vocabulary: Define each of the following completely.

1. Red Herring: ***An obvious distraction from the main issue.***

2. Appeal to Ignorance: ***Abusing the "burden of proof" by making your opponent irrefutably prove their position rather than making a sound argument for your own.***

3. Irrelevant Goals or Functions: ***Judging something to be ineffective on the basis of a goal or function that it wasn't intended to fulfill.***

4. Irrelevant Thesis: ***An argument proving the wrong point.***

5. Straw Man Fallacy: ***Arguing against an unfair and inaccurate portrayal of an opponent's position.***

B. Identification:
Which Red Herring Argument is being described below? Explain your answer.

My parents have always told me to stay away from drugs and alcohol. They've pointed out that getting caught-up in a lifestyle that includes drugs and alcohol has usually hindered a person's ability to reach high standards and goals. Now that I'm on my own and in college, I think it's time that I stop doing exactly what mom and dad tell me, and start making my own decisions. If I rely on my parents to decide everything for me, I won't learn how to be a responsible adult. They shouldn't tell me what to do any more.

So, the next time someone offers me something to drink or smoke, I won't automatically say "no" because my parent's say so. I'm going to wait and make my own decision when the time comes. I might accept their offer, but that's okay. Because, I'm making my own decisions and I'm going to learn responsibility from asserting independence.

irrelevant thesis

C. Application:
Name all four types of Red Herring Arguments. Then, create or find two examples of each

The Art of Argument

CUMULATIVE FALLACY WORKSHEET III

DIRECTIONS: under each example, write both the category and the specific fallacy.

1. As far as I'm concerned, the Medicaid program is a total waste. There are still people in this country who go without care because they're uninsured.
   irrelevant goals and functions

2. You shouldn't put any stock in the accusations made against the President. They were only the result of the over-zealousness of reporters that were out to make names for themselves.
   either ***ad hominem circumstantial*** *(since it refers to the self-interest of the speakers) or* ***irrelevant thesis***, *since it is undoubtedly true that they are out to make names for themselves, but not the key issue.*

3. **Senator Jones:** I support legislation banning abortion or even a Constitutional amendment if necessary. A civilized society simply cannot stomach the killing of so many innocent children.

   Senator Smith: If you're so concerned about the sanctity of life, why won't you join me in my opposition to the death penalty?
   irrelevant thesis

4. Representative Johnston has no grounds making any judgement about the President. It's been proven that he's an adulterer himself.
   tu quoque

5. I don't see how any good Christian can celebrate Christmas. It's nothing more than an attempt to Christianize the old Pagan festivals of the Winter Solstice.
   genetic fallacy

6. **Scully:** So far you haven't presented me any solid evidence of this government conspiracy that you're referring to.
   Mulder: And you haven't found anything to definitely disprove it.
   appeal to ignorance

7. Ladies and gentlemen, do you really want these bigoted Christian fundamentalists to be running things! Don't let them bring their religious jihad here to Central Dauphin School District. Vote against Jackson, Andrews and Noll for school board.
   ad hominem abusive

8. Hindus don't believe in helping the poor. That's why Hinduism is a religion of callous inhumanity. All one has to do is walk the streets of India to see how little Hindus care about the plight of those less fortunate.
   straw man

9. **Reporter:** Mr. President, do you think that your age ought to be a factor in the voter's decision in November?
The President: No I don't think age ought to be a factor. After all, I've never made an issue of my opponent's age and inexperience.
irrelevant thesis

. . . .

Exercise
Chapter 6.1: The Fallacies of Presumption

Can you detect the way in which the following argument "begs the question" to remain hidden?

> People of good literary taste have established that Shakespeare is the best poet to have ever written in the English Language. To find a person of good literary taste all you need confirm is that he recognizes Shakespeare as the greatest English poet the world has ever seen.

This argument assumes what it sets out to prove—that people of good literary taste think Shakespeare is the best English poet. Is it possible that someone with good literary taste will not think Shakespeare is the best English poet? Not if you assume that such a person must think Shakespeare is the best English poet to be considered a person of good literary taste!

. . . .

Review Exercise
Chapter 6.9: The Fallacies of Presumption

A. Define. In cases of Latin terms, also give the translation:

1. Fallacies of Presupposition: *Arguments that are flawed because they are based on hidden and unjustified assumptions*

2. Fallacies of Presumption: *Arguments that are flawed because they presume unjustified assumptions or violate the principles of inductive reasoning.*

3. Axioms: *Foundational principles upon which an argument rests.*

4. Enthymeme: *An argument in which at least one statement is assumed rather than explicitly stated.*

5. Begging the Question: *An argument that is flawed because it "begs" more questions than it answers.*

The Art of Argument

6. Bifurcation: *An argument which assumes that only two choices are possible, when, in fact, there may be other possible options.*

7. Dilemma: *A situation in which only two (generally unpleasant) possibilities are possible.*

8. Fallacy of Moderation: *An argument which assumes that truth or morality is always found in compromise.*

9. Is-Ought Fallacy: *An argument that assumes that just because something is a certain way that it ought to be.*

10. Fallacy of Composition: *A fallacy that assumes that a collective whole will necessarily have the same characteristics as its parts.*

11. Fallacy of Division: *A fallacy that assumes that the parts of a collective whole will have the same characteristics as the whole.*

B. Identification: Determine which fallacy is being used in each of the following examples.

1. The speaker makes the assumption that the parts will have the same properties as a collective whole.
   division

2. The speaker is either just restating the conclusion in other words or uses a justification that is more controversial than the original conclusion.
   begging the question

3. The speaker assumes that a collective whole will have the properties of the sum of its parts.
   composition

4. The speaker assumes that something is the right thing simply because it is the way that things are.
   is-ought

5. The speaker assumes that the best solution to a problem is necessarily a compromise between extremes.
   moderation

6. The speaker assumes that only two possibilities exist, when in fact there may be others.
   bifurcation

C. In Depth: Name which Fallacy of Presumption is being committed in the following examples. Explain your answers.

1. Now you think that the problem is mostly your wife's fault and your wife thinks it is mostly your fault. Let's just start out by admitting that there's probably an equal amount of blame on each side.
   moderation

2. Look, either you accept that we need full funding for the V-22 Osprey, or admit that you don't have the best interests of our national defense at heart.
   bifurcation

3. Logos Christian School is the finest Christian school in the Chattanooga area! You ask how I can state this with such confidence? Easy: we have an all-star staff.
   composition

4. Luc Longley is just the ingredient that the Phoenix Suns need to win a championship. Everyone conceded that the center position has been their achilles heel since time immemorial and Luc has started at center for all six championship seasons of the incomparable Chicago Bulls.
   division (just because the Bulls were a great team, doesn't mean they had a great center.)

5. Failure to support our public schools is a failure to support education, because that is how America is educated!
   is-ought fallacy. (just because that is how Americans are generally educated that way, doesn't mean they ought to be.)

6. Of course I can't support public education. It's nothing more than a big-government monopoly.
   begging the question (the assertion that big-government monopolies are a bad way to educate must first be argued.)

. . . .

CUMULATIVE FALLACY WORKSHEET IV

DIRECTIONS: Under each example, write both the category and the specific fallacy.

1. What do you mean the Palestinians shouldn't have their own state? They've never had a state before, they don't have one now and that's how things ought to be.
   is-ought. (The speaker is confusing the way that a situation is for the way that it should be. It could also possibly be called an appeal to tradition.)

The Art of Argument

2. **Johnny Darwin:** Surely you must see that life follows inexorably the principle of "Survival of the Fittest."
   Billy Bryan: Well, in that case, how do we know which are the fittest?
   Johnny Darwin: Why, they are the ones that survive.
   Billy Bryan: Well, what do you mean by "fittest."
   Johnny Darwin: Why, I mean the set of qualities which best enable one to survive.
   begging the question (this is a classic case of a circular argument; since it also concerns the definition of the term "fittest" it's also a sort of question-begging definition. Note that, used in this way by Darwinists, the term "fittest" is often equivocated on.)

3. In the road of life, there are passengers and there are drivers. Drivers wanted. (Volkswagen commercial.)
   bifurcation and snob appeal

4. We can't possibly believe that the Vice President's energy program is in the best interests of the country. He's a former executive for a prominent energy company.
   ad hominem circumstantial

5. The marines did a great job in Afghanistan. They're a great organization. We need to hire one for our security company.
   division (just because the marines as a whole are very effective doesn't mean that an individual marine is going to be the best man for the job.)

6. The best and brightest always read the *New York Times*.
   snob appeal

7. Look, the Palestinians want all of the land and the Israelis want all of the land, so let's just compromise and give each groups exactly half.
   moderation (a 50/50 split isn't always the most just solution)

8. How can you oppose this bill? Either you support this bill or you do not have the safety of the American people at heart.
   bifurcation

9. Create a lighter-than-air vehicle!? That's impossible. I've never once seen anything that is lighter than air that someone could make a vehicle out of!
   composition (the vehicle as a whole can be lighter than air even if individual pieces aren't

10. How can support Senator Jones' bill? He's nothing but a debauched, drunken idiot!
    ad hominem abusive

11. How can Senator Bruce support this bill against drunken driving? He's been convicted of drunk driving himself.
    tu quoque

The Art ∫

Exercises
Chapter 7.1: Sweeping Generalization

How can Inductive Arguments be weak?

1. **The evidence could be incomplete, lacking one or more critical facts.**

2. **The evidence could be distorted, causing the argument to be deceptively weak.**

. . . .

Exercises
Chapter 7.4: False Analogy

Identify each analogy below as either a good or bad analogy and explain why.

1. Providing a laptop to every college student is a bad idea. That would be like giving them a free pass to an arcade.

    Bad Analogy—Computers, while they do have games on them, are not similar to arcades.

2. Giving a laptop to every college freshmen is an excellent idea. Every workman performs better with the best tools.

    Good Analogy—A computer is very much like a tool.

3. Reading a great book is like making a new friend.

    Good Analogy—Books are often the presentation in writing of a person.

4. We shouldn't cut anyone from the basketball team anymore than we should excuse students from P.E. class.

    Bad Analogy—P.E. is usually a required class, basketball is not.

5. Ethics is like art—you have to draw a line somewhere.

    Good in one limited respect that is also metaphorical.

The Art

Review Exercises
Chapter 7.6: The Fallacies of Induction

A. Define: In cases of Latin terms, also give the translation:

1. Sweeping Generalization: *An argument that assumes that a generalization is always true.*

2. Hasty Generalization: *An argument that forms a generalization on the basis of too few examples.*

3. False Analogy: *An argument that draws a conclusion about one situation on the basis of another, even though the two things being compared aren't similar enough in the right way.*

4. False Cause: *An argument based on inadequate causal reasoning.*

5. Fake Precision: *An argument based on the misuse of statistics.*

B. Examples: Name the fallacy committed in the following examples. State reasons why you believe your answers to be correct.

1. I saw Bobby putting gum under the table. Jimmy is a young teenager too, so I think that if I give him a piece of gum, he'll do the same thing.
   false analogy (Note that the reason is moving from one specific case to another specific case.)

2. Since Jimmy and Bobby both stuck their gum under the table, we can be pretty sure that any teenager would do the same.
   hasty generalization (Note that the reasoning is moving from two examples toward a generalization.

3. Studies show that 90% of teenagers stick their gum under the table when given the opportunity. Therefore, we can be pretty sure that Susie will do the same. (note: ignore the bogus study and what fallacy remains.)
   sweeping generalization (Note that the reasoning is moving from a generalization to one specific case.)

4. The average person tells a lie every 12 hours.
   fake precision

5. Every time the copier breaks down, it always seems to be right after you use it. You must be jinxing it.
   false cause

C. In Depth: Find 3 examples of Fake Precision. Use recent newspapers, magazines or web sites articles. Be prepared to discuss how and why the example uses the fallacy of Fake Precision.

. . . .

CUMULATIVE FALLACY WORKSHEET V

DIRECTIONS: Under each example, write both the category and the specific fallacy.

1. Don't tell me your sob stories about terrorism. You Americans killed plenty of innocent civilians during the campaign in Afghanistan.
   Presumption, false analogy (sad as accidental casualties are, they are a very different thing from the deliberate targeting of civilians)

2. I've always been favorably disposed toward those named Jonathan. That's the name of my wonderful brother and I've never known someone named Jonathan that wasn't a pretty good guy.
   Presumption, hasty generalization (the sample size is likely too small)

3. You simply can't convict this man! Think of his wife, of his children, crying even now in this courtroom and pining at home without him if you choose to send him off to jail.
   Relevance, appeal to pity

4. "Official sources indicate that an attack against Iraq is nearly certain before year's end."
   Relevance, appeal to illegitimate authority (Since the sources are unknown it would be unwise to take the reporters word for it.)

5. You can't give Dr. Jones' theories any credence. He's not a real scholar! He's just a journalistic hack! Why, I wouldn't be surprised if he got his degree out of a Cracker Jack box.
   Relevance, ad hominem abusive

6. Lowenbrau—A German tradition!
   Relevance, chronological snobbery (appeal to tradition)

7. I went to a chiropractor and he didn't help me. Those guys are just a bunch of quacks.
   Presumption, hasty generalization (not enough information)

8. I don't care if that guy weighed 300 lbs.! You're a Boy Scout and Boy Scouts help those in need! You should have jumped right on into that lake to try to save him!
   Presumption, sweeping generalization (it might be a good general rule to jump in and save a drowning man, but there are exceptions when there is no chance that it could be done w/o having him pull you under as well. A better tactic would be to look for a life preserver or get help.)

9. Every time I let you borrow my car, it breaks down. You must be jinxing it!
   Presumption, false cause

The Art

10. Hey, I know that Mussolini's rise to power was a bit brutal, but hey, you can't make an omelet without breaking a few eggs.
  Presumption, false analogy *(people aren't eggs)*

. . . .

Review Exercises
Chapter 8.6: The Fallacies of Clarity

A. Define: In cases of Latin terms, also give the translation:

1. Fallacies of Clarity: ***Fallacies that result from language that is ambiguous or confusing***

2. Equivocation: ***Fallacies that result when a key term shifts in its meaning.***

3. Accent: ***Fallacies that result when a word or phrase is improperly emphasized or taken out of context.***

4. Distinction without Difference: ***Fallacies that result when someone tries to distinguish two things that aren't really different.***

B. Vocabulary Review: Name the fallacy that is being described by the following definitions.

1. Ambiguity that is created by the fact that a word has more than one meaning is...
  equivocation

2. Confusion that is created by misplaced stress on one particular word or syllable is...
  fallacy of accent

3. Confusion caused by treating a purely semantic distinction is if it were a real distinction.
  distinction with out a difference

C. Examples: Name the fallacy that is being described by the following examples. State reasons why you believe your answer to be correct.

1. But Mom, you said that I shouldn't take any cookies. That's why I'm eating them right here by the cookie jar.
  accent (on "take")

2. Dagwood isn't really lazy. He just likes to sleep all the time.

The Art

distinction without a difference

3. The paparazzi always seem to get a bum rap. What they are doing is clearly in the public interest. After all, if it wasn't, pictures and information about celebrities wouldn't be such a profitable commodity.
equivocation (on the word "interest")

4. God is that which nothing greater can be conceived. Something which exists in the mind is greater than something that is imaginary. Therefore, the One True God must necessarily exist.
This might be a somewhat controversial conclusion, but I see this as an equivocation on the word "God." He (Anselm) starts out with a stipulative definition for "God" but what he really means by "God" in the end is the God he knows, the God of Abraham, Isaac and Jacob.

. . . .

CUMULATIVE FALLACY WORKSHEET VI
DIRECTIONS: Under each example, write both the category and the specific fallacy.

1. Take it easy, boss! It's not that I'm just standing around. I'm supervising!
Clarity, distinction without a difference

2. The world couldn't have been created by God, because matter has always existed and therefore there is no need for a Creator-God.
Presumption, begging the question (the question of whether matter has always existed is precisely that which is at issue)

3. **Johnny Darwin:** It is clear that man is descended from the apes.
Billy Bryan: So on which side of the family are you descended from the apes, your mother's side or your father's side?
Relevance, ad hominem abusive (Bryan deflects the issue by ridiculing his opponent.)

4. Want war? Vote for Goldwater!
Relevance, appeal to fear

5. The end of a thing is its perfection. Death is the end of life; therefore it is life's perfection.
Clarity, equivocation (on the word "end." End can either mean simply chronological end or it can mean goal. When we say that death is the end of life, we generally mean the former, not the latter.)

6. Socialism is clearly the only way to fully realize the principles of the Declaration of Independence, for does it not say that all men are created equal? Socialism is the only system that recognizes the natural human yearning for equality by mandating that "from each according to his ability, to each according to his need." Only socialism tries to make sure that equality extends to the realm of economics!
Clarity, equivocation again (on "equality" The Declaration didn't intend to mean that all

The Art

men are
created equal in every material aspect, but rather in their political rights.)

7. **Mom:** "Billy, you need to be polite to your uncle!"
   Billy: "But Mom, you told me to be courteous to strangers."
   Clarity, accent

8. He's not really a criminal. He just likes to "borrow" a few items now and then from the store.
   Relevance, distinction without a difference

9. I don't believe you! You're just a meany-head!
   Relevance, ad hominem abusive

10. Why do you want to major in history? You already said that you don't want to be a teacher.
    Relevance, irrelevant goals and functions *(Teaching history is not the only reason why one might want to major in history.)*

The Art

Quiz: Ad Fontem Argument

1. Definitions:

Directions: label each of the following definitions with the fallacy with most closely fits its from the following list: ***ad hominem abusive, ad hominem circumstantial, and tu quoque***

This fallacy occurs when...

1. ... The speaker asserts that because of the self -interest of or the circumstances surrounding his rival, his rival's arguments should be discounted.

2. ... The speaker asserts that we should discount his rival's argument because his rival has not been entirely consistent in either advocating or practicing it.

3. ... The speaker says all sorts of mean and nasty things about his rival as evidence that his rival's argument should be discounted.

4. ... An idea is discounted only because of its origin.

II. EXAMPLES: (Name the fallacy committed in the example below.)

1. Don't listen to him. He's a no-good, dirty rotten scoundrel.

2. I don't believe you; you got that information from The Nation and that's just a liberal rag.

3. How can you tell me to "just say no," today, Dad, when you said yes in the 60's?

4. Why should I give any weight to your arguments for legal reform? You're a lawyer and probably stand to benefit from such reforms.

CUMULATIVE FALLACY QUIZ I

I. DEFINITIONS:

PART A: Name the fallacy that is described.

1. A speaker tries to convince us by making us feel sorry for himself or others.

2. An appeal to various bad consequences that will follow if one doesn't accept the speaker's argument, without showing a clear causal link.

3. Implying that two wrongs make a right by discounting someone's argument solely on the basis that they are not entirely consistent.

4. Appealing to the emotions of a crowd or to the common man to make up for a lack of solid evidence or sound reasoning.

5. Discounting a rival's argument solely on the basis of certain circumstances surrounding them.

PART B: Define the following fallacies.

1. SNOB APPEAL:

2. AD HOMINEM ABUSIVE:

3. GENETIC FALLACY:

II. EXAMPLES:

Directions: Write both the general category and the specific fallacy committed under each example. *Remember*: Give the reason why you picked the answer that you picked in order to get partial credit.

1. You have no right to speak on the issue of poverty; you've never been poor, so you don't know what it's like.

2. It's clear that Al D'Amato's investigation of the president was just a partisan attack. What else would you expect from such a vain and vindictive man. Him losing the election was great for New York.

3. Of course those legislators from North Carolina are against this tobacco regulation only because they're in the pockets of the industry. You can't take any of their arguments seriously.

4. If you don't speak up for the oppressed minorities in this country, by enacting legislation against hate crimes, prejudice and violence will increase.

5. You really ought to take Jen to the prom, Jon. I know that you're not dating her anymore,

but just think of how sad and lonely she'll be all alone at home on the night of her senior prom.

6. I know it was dumb to jump out of a moving car, Nathan, but you did it too.

7. Since the Christian Coalition's opinions derive from religious convictions, their views should have no place in the public square, since we believe in a separation of church and state in this country.

8. Please trust that I have the best ideas for furthering the interests of working families in all of my policies, because I feel your pain.

9. Ladies and gentlemen, accepting Jesus into your heart is like buying an eternal life insurance policy to protect you from the fires of Hell. Look, even if you're wrong, and Christianity is false, it won't do you any harm. And if you don't, well, then, you just might be awfully sorry come the judgement day.

CUMULATIVE FALLACY QUIZ II

I. DEFINITIONS:

PART A: Under each definition, list the fallacy that most closely represents it.

1. An appeal to the mere fact that a belief is widely held to prove its truth.

2. The classic trick of the demagogue, this fallacy is an appeal to the mystique of the "common man", or the "working man".

3. This is an appeal to those of "discriminating tastes."

4. This fallacy occurs when the speaker depends on emotional appeals to make his audience feel sorry for himself or others in the place of sound evidence.

5. This is an illegitimate appeal to the opinion of an expert. The most common situations in which this occurs are when the expert is not named, is biased or when he is not really an expert in the field in question.

6. This is an appeal to the mere age of a belief or practice as evidence that it is correct.

PART B: Beside each fallacy name, write the definition of the fallacy.

1. AD HOMINEM ABUSIVE

2. AD HOMINEM CIRCUMSTANTIAL

3. TU QUOQUE

4. GENETIC FALLACY

II. EXAMPLES:

1. Check out the Ford F-150; it's the best selling vehicle in America.

2. Yuengling Lager: made by the oldest brewery in America.

3. Anyone opposing the legislation concerning zero emissions vehicles cannot possibly have the welfare of our environment at heart.

4. Twin Brooks Winery: no other Lancaster County winery has dedicated itself to producing the classic French varietals with such single-minded devotion. Only the best grapes make it into our bottles.

5. Hi, I'm Tom Hanks. I've got a great idea. Why don't we all just respect each other's differences. Wouldn't that be a great political platform.

6. People who know cars use Valvoline!

7. Our educational system is in crisis right now and you suggest we engage in risky experiments with untried ideas like vouchers. Surely you don't want our educational system to collapse around our ears and leave us all without enough schools to educate our children!

8. Ladies and gentlemen, those who are opposed to this measure are the lowest kind of base cowards that could possibly be imagined. Do no allow their silly indecisiveness to influence your voting.

9. Back in the days of slavery, they had an old saying. There were those slaves who had the privilege of living in the house and in order to get this privilege, they had to serve the master the way he wanted to be served. Colin Powel is like one of those house slaves serving his

master, George Bush, faithfully, but if he steps out of line, he might be sent back into the fields. (Paraphrased from statements by Harry Belefante.)

10. How can George Bush have any credibility when speaking of the dangers of alcohol? He admits to having had alcohol problems himself.

III. OPTIONAL SUPPLEMENT ON APPEALS TO AUTHORITY:

Directions: for each of the examples below, name which of the five tests for appeals to authority it fails.

1. "According to sources close to the President, he is prepared to resign if articles of impeachment are passed."

2. Hi, I'm Dan Marino. If you need a loan, let me tell you, you won't get a better deal than what you'll get from the folks at the Money Store.

3. Dr. Stone has a PhD in Economics and he says the Dow Jones Industrial is going to drop 600 points next year, so you better cash in your stocks as soon as possible.

4. There's no such thing as flying squirrels. My big brother said so, so there!

5. According to the Rainbow Coalition, we need more money to save our public schools, so if you don't agree that we ought to raise taxes, then you obviously don't care about education.

6. My dad's a scientist and he says Creationism is bunk, so he must be right.

Red Herrings Logic Quiz:

I. DEFINITIONS:

1. IRRELEVANT THESIS:

2. IRRELEVANT GOALS/ FUNCTIONS:

3. STRAW MAN:

4. APPEAL TO IGNORANCE:

II. EXAMPLES:

1. Why are you so insistent on asking for proof that there is a ghost haunting the widow Maloney's mansion? You haven't given me any proof that there isn't.

2. I can't support the impeachment of the president. The people supporting it are just a bunch of people obsessed with getting the President on any little thing they can find.

3. President Reagan: "Don't make age an issue in this campaign. After all, I've never raised the issue of my opponent's youth and inexperience."

4. Don't give me all those old tired lines about being pro life. You're for the death penalty and that's not pro-life.

5. If you cannot absolutely disprove my atheism by giving an airtight argument for the

existence of God that I can accept, then the only logical conclusion that can be reached is that we should live our lives as though there is no God.

6. Why would you major in history?   You don't want to teach history, so you wouldn't have a very marketable job.

7. Taoism doesn't make any sense. All it is is a bunch of trite obvious sayings said with a certain rhetorical gravity so they impress the gullible into thinking that they are profound.

8. A Puritan is someone who is terribly afraid that somewhere, somehow, someone might be having some fun.

CUMULATIVE LOGIC QUIZ III

I. DEFINITIONS:

PART A: This fallacy results from...

1. ... arguing against a caricatured or exaggerated version of an opponent's position.

2. ...arguing that because someone cannot disprove our position that it must be right.

3. ...calling our opponent all sorts of nasty names rather than challenging his argument.

4. ...proving a different point than the one that is relevant to the issue at hand.

5. ...accepting an illegitimate appeal to the authority of an expert.

6. ...arguing that a practice is not the right one because it doesn't fulfill a purpose for which it was never intended.

PART B: Give the definition for each fallacy below.

1. AD HOMINEM CIRCUMSTANTIAL:

2. MOB APPEAL:

3. SNOB APPEAL:

4. CHRONOLOGICAL SNOBBERY:

5. GENETIC FALLACY:

6. TU QUOQUE

II. EXAMPLES:

1. How can the prosecution seriously suggest that my client committed this brutal crime? He's a fine, upstanding pillar of this community and a dedicated family man loved by all.

2. The only reason why you oppose this badly-needed reform measure for reporting corporate income is because you're an accountant and you have much to gain by the current system.

3. Feminists like her only believe in women's lib because they hate men.

4. Christmas is a pagan, Roman, commercialized holiday. Christians shouldn't celebrate it.

5. Don't major in philosophy. My father used to say that when you're sick, you go to a doctor, when you're in trouble you need a lawyer, but every man has his own philosophy!

6. Don't tell me that I can't prove that the president has been involved in multiple murder conspiracies. You can't prove that he isn't.

7. There's nothing wrong with polygamy. After all, it was practiced in even the oldest civilizations of which we have records.

LOGIC QUARTERFINAL I
(Unit 1)

I. DEFINITIONS:

1. AD HOMINEM ABUSIVE:

2. AD HOMINEM CIRCUMSTANTIAL:

3. TU QUOQUE:

4. GENETIC FALLACY:

5. APPEAL TO FEAR:

6. APPEAL TO PITY:

7. MOB APPEAL:

8. APPEAL TO ILLEGITIMATE AUTHORITY:

9. SNOB APPEAL:

10. CHRONOLOGICAL SNOBBERY:

11. APPEAL TO IGNORANCE:

12. IRRELEVANT THESIS:

13. IRRELEVANT GOALS AND FUNCTIONS:

14. STRAW MAN:

II. EXAMPLES:

A. PERSONAL ATTACKS/ AD FONTEM ARGUMENTS

1. I can't believe that you would give his ideas any credence. He's nothing but a long-haired, maggot-infested, dope-smoking, FM type.

2. You only favor a capital gains tax cut because you own lots of stock and stand to benefit.

3. The only reason that you believe in God is because you have felt a need for a father figure and have built a wish projection onto reality for a paternal God.

4. Why did you put my name on the board for talking? Everyone else was talking too.

B. EMOTIONAL APPEALS

1. Don't vote for these country-club, blue-blooded Republicans. Vote for John Jackson, champion of the American working man.

2. Those Gingrich Republicans are the ones you should beware of. They're coming for our children, they're coming for the elderly...

3. Esteemed members of Congress, have pity on the poor American taxpayer, taxed more than at any other time in history. Please, gentlemen, lighten his load by accepting this tax cut proposal.

4. Cars do so run on water! My big brother told me so, so there!

5. Smoke Camel Regulars: they're the real man's cigarette.

6. Polygamy must be OK, since it goes back as far back as recorded history.

7. Buy a Ford F-150, the best-selling vehicle in America!

C. RED HERRINGS

1. I don't see why we're spending so much on the so-called "war on drugs". Alcohol is far more frequently abused and it's still legal.

2. Our political opponents have challenged us to give them evidence that there really is a "health-care crisis." Well I ask them to give us some evidence that there isn't.

3. Those Christian Right activists are just a bunch of homophobes who encourage violence against homosexuals.

4. Let's get serious here, gentlemen; giving the American people a tax cut is not going to solve all of their financial problems.

CUMULATIVE FALLACY QUIZ IV

I. DEFINITIONS:

Part A: *This fallacy is committed when...*

1. ...the speaker makes the assumption that the parts will have the same properties as a collective whole.

2. ...the speaker is either just restating the conclusion in other words or uses a justification that is more controversial than the original conclusion.

3. ...the speaker assumes that a collective whole will have the properties of the sum of its parts.

4. ...the speaker assumes that something is the right thing simply because it is the way that things happen to be.

5. ...the speaker assumes that the best solution to a problem is necessarily a compromise between extremes.

6. ...the speaker assumes that only two possibilities exist, when in fact there may be others.

Part B: Give the definition for the fallacy named.

1. AD HOMINEM ABUSIVE

2. GENETIC FALLACY

3. APPEAL TO ILLEGITIMATE AUTHORITY

4. TU QUOQUE

5. STRAW MAN

6. IRRELEVANT GOALS/ FUNCITONS

7. IRRELEVANT THESIS

8. CHRONOLOGICAL SNOBBERY

II. EXAMPLES:

1. Look, if those Bosnian Serbs and Muslims can't live together, why don't we just split the land in half and give half to each of them?

2. No Christian can, in good conscience, serve in the military. One can either be a man of peace or a man of war and the Christian's Lord is the Prince of Peace.

3. Look: I'm a soldier because that is what I am. That is what I've always been and it's all that I know.

4. "These three musketeers are valiant men, and consummate swordsmen. If I had an army of such men, we would be unstoppable!"

5. **Mr. Engleton:** Dickens' works are much better literature than those of Tolkien.
   Johnny: How does one know which works are great literature?
   Mr. Engleton: They are the ones recommended by the well-informed.
   Johnny: How does one get to be well-informed?
   Mr. Engleton: Why, by reading great works of literature like Dickens, of course.

6. The men who wrote this program had worked for Microsoft, the most powerful, successful, hard-driving company in the software industry. They must have been great programmers themselves.

FALLACIES OF INDUCTION QUIZ

I. DEFINITIONS:

PART A: Give the fallacy of induction that best fits the following description.

1. Basing an argument on a comparison of two examples that don't have enough similarity.

2. Creating a generalization on the basis of too few examples.

3. Basing an argument on a weak causal connection.

4. Extending a generalization to exceptional cases.

5. The misuse of statistics

PART B: Give the definition for the fallacy named below:

1. FALLACY OF COMPOSITION

2. FALLACY OF MODERATION

3. IS-OUGHT FALLACY

4. BIFURCATION

5. BEGGING THE QUESTION

6. FALLACY OF DIVISION

7. TU QUOQUE

8. STRAW MAN

9. CHRONOLOGICAL SNOBBERY

II. EXAMPLES: (Careful: there's one Fallacy of Presupposition buried in here to keep you on your toes)!

1. It's no wonder that violent crime has increased lately, what with all those violent Hollywood movies they make lately!

2. We shouldn't let kids watch those violent Hollywood movies because it just isn't right for them to see such images of brutality and hurtfulness.

3. After all, people who watch violent movies have 4 times as many violent thoughts as those who do not.

4. You know that guy Tommy watches violent movies all the time and he gets into fights all the time, so it's obvious that violent movies cause people to be violent.

5. Since people who watch violent movies are four times as likely to commit violent crimes, Jon-boy is more likely to commit one if he watches such movies. (Assume that these numbers are based on a legitimate study).

6. Since that guy Tommy gets into fights and he watches violent movies, Johnny will do just the same if he watches violent movies.

7. OK, so you've finally conceded that Stallone movies are too violent. Three Stooges movies are out too, because of all the hitting and striking that goes on in those violent flicks.

CUMULATIVE FALLACY QUIZ V

I. DEFINITIONS:

1. BEGGING THE QUESTION:

2. BIFURCATION/FALSE DILEMMA:

3. FALLACY OF MODERATION:

4. FALLACY OF COMPOSITION:

5. FALLACY OF DIVISION:

6. IS-OUGHT FALLACY:

7. SWEEPING GENERALIZATION (ACCIDENT):

8. HASTY GENERALIZATION (CONVERSE ACCIDENT):

9. FALSE ANALOGY:

10. FALSE CAUSE:

11. FAKE PRECISION:

II. EXAMPLES:

PART A: Select from the following three possibilities: *False Analogy, Hasty Generalization, Sweeping Generalization*

1. People who make bad grades usually do so because they do not study. Since Jack is making bad grades, it's obvious that he doesn't study.

2. John admits that his problems in school are a result of a lack of effort. Jack is struggling, too, so that must be his problem, too.

3. John and Susie just don't try very hard at school. Kids these days are just so lazy.

PART B: Select from the following possibilities: *False Cause, Fake Precision, Composition and Division.*

1. Dennis Rodman is a great basketball player. When they add him to Shaquille O'Neal and Kobe Bryant, they are sure to have a great team.

2. Any law against partial birth abortion will be very unpopular. After all, a recent study by the People for the American Way showed that 82% of people believe in reproductive rights for women.

3. Studies show that most elementary school teachers are parents. It must be because working with children stimulates an interest in parenthood.

4. John Elway needs to be elected MVP of the NFL. After all, his team is the best team in the league right now.

PART C: Select from the following possibilities: *Begging the Question, Is-ought, Bifurcation, Moderation*

1. Of course abortion is OK. It's a legal activity, isn't it?

2. The solution to the Kosovo crisis is obvious: why don't the Serbs just give Kosovo the same status as Montinegro, as a separate republic within Yugoslavia. Then the Serbs and Albanians could just compromise and get along.

3. Since you started 8 months ago, you have consistently had the lowest sales in the Department. If you haven't figured out what your problem is, you obviously don't understand the business. If you have figured it out and haven't corrected it, you don't learn from your mistakes. Either way, you are a proven failure as an employee and we can't afford to keep such people on the payroll.

4. We need a Women's History month because women need a special time to celebrate their own achievements.

PART D: Select from the following possibilities: *Hasty Generalization, Sweeping Generalization, Composition and Division.*

1. That blimp is a lighter than air vehicle. That must mean that everything on it is lighter than air.

2. People who live on Lookout Mountain are mostly pretty wealthy. Your friend Greg lives on Lookout Mountain, so he must be loaded.

3. Jon, Mike and I are not as athletic as those guys. There's no way we could put together a team that could beat them.

4. My Uncle Harry is a crazy driver. It must be a quality common to all people from Queens.

CUMULATIVE FALLACY QUIZ VI

I. DEFINITIONS:

1. Ambiguity that is created by the fact that a word has more than one meaning is...

2. Confusion that is created by misplaced stress on one particular word or syllable is...

3. Confusion caused by treating a purely semantic distinction as if it were a real distinction.

II. EXAMPLES:

1. He said that this dress looks good on me. I can't believe he would imply that the other doesn't.

2. Mr. Jones must be a very responsible person. If anything goes wrong at Lewis Academy, he is held responsible.

3. Jack isn't an angry person. He just flies into a rage and hurts people every once in a while.

III. REVIEW DEFINITIONS:

1. BEGGING THE QUESTION:

2. BIFURCATION/FALSE DILEMMA:

3. FALLACY OF MODERATION:

4. FALLACY OF COMPOSITION:

5. FALLACY OF DIVISION:

6. IS-OUGHT FALLACY:

7. SWEEPING GENERALIZATION (ACCIDENT):

8. HASTY GENERALIZATION (CONVERSE ACCIDENT):

9. FALSE ANALOGY:

10. FALSE CAUSE:

11. FAKE PRECISION:

LOGIC QUARTERFINAL II
(Unit II)

I. DEFINITIONS: Write out the definitions for the following fallacies.

1. EQUIVOCATION:

2. ACCENT:

3. DISTINCTION WITHOUT A DIFFERENCE:

II. DEFINITIONS: Name which fallacy goes with the following definitions

1. Making a generalization based on too few examples is...

2. Building an argument based on a comparison of two things that ought not be compared is...

3. Applying a generalization to exceptional circumstances that it ought not apply to is...

4. Drawing conclusions about a collective whole based on the characteristics of the parts is...

5. Drawing conclusions about the parts of a collective whole based on the characteristics of the whole is...

6. Making an argument that is either circular or rests on premises that are more controversial than the conclusions is...

7. Misusing statistics is...

8. Building an argument on a weak causal connection is...

9. Assuming that the truth is always a middle ground between extremes is...

10. Building an argument on a false dilemma is...

11. Assuming that something is right simply because it happens to be that way is...

III. EXAMPLES: Choose from the following: *hasty generalization, sweeping generalization and false analogy*

1. English majors are legendary for not being good at math. Gordon was an English major, so he's not going to do well in my college Algebra class.

2. Scott wasn't very good at math. English majors must not be very talented at it.

3. Since Scott, an English major, did poorly at math, it's obvious that Gordon, an English major as well, will have trouble.

IV EXAMPLES: Choose from the following: *Begging the Question, Equivocation, Distinction Without a Difference, Accent and Bifurcation.*

1. There are laws of nature. Laws imply a lawgiver. Therefore, there must be a Cosmic lawgiver.

2. There are two types of people in the world: those who own Mercedes-Benz automobiles and those who wish they did.

3. There is no such thing as knowledge which cannot be put into practice, for such knowledge is no knowledge at all. (Confucius)

4. Only Hollywood could produce a film like this.

5. I'm not a poor student. I just don't study very hard.

V. EXAMPLES: Choose from the following: *Hasty Generalization, Sweeping Generalization, Composition and Division.*

1. Cars put out less pollution than buses. Therefore, an increase in emphasis on busing will also increase pollution levels.

2. Weiss Markets has a lower price on milk and eggs than Giant. I'll save money if I shop there.

3. Studies show that taking regular doses of Vitamin C can prevent sickness. If I take these vitamin pills, I should stay healthy.

4. The Roman legions dominated the battlefield for 400 years. The legionaries must have been the best warriors of their time.

VI EXAMPLES: Choose from the following: *False Cause, Fake Precision, Fallacy of Moderation and Is-ought Fallacy.*

1. You said that one must come to class, participate in discussion and read the material in order to do well in the class. I did all of these things, and yet I only got a C. Why?

2. "Mr. and Mrs. Cain; I know that you're going through a rough patch in your relationship. Let's just begin by admitting that you are both probably in the wrong on many things."

3. Public Affairs is not really the most important thing for a president to spend his time on. The public doesn't seem to care that much and the administration treats it as an afterthought.

4. When the average salary of all men and all women is factored, the women's average is only $.74 to every dollar that men earn.

QUIZ: Ad Fontem Arguments

I. DEFINITIONS:

Directions: label each of the following definitions with the fallacy with most closely fits its from the following list: ***ad hominem abusive, ad hominem circumstantial, and tu quoque***

This fallacy occurs when...

1. ... The speaker asserts that because of the self-interest of or the circumstances surrounding his rival, his rival's arguments should be discounted.
ad hominem circumstantial

2. ... The speaker asserts that we should discount his rival's argument because his rival has not been entirely consistent in either advocating or practicing it.
tu quoque

3. ... The speaker says all sorts of mean and nasty things about his rival as evidence that his rival's argument should be discounted.
ad hominem abusive

4. ... An idea is discounted only because of its origin.
genetic fallacy

II. EXAMPLES: (Name the fallacy committed in the example below.)

1. Don't listen to him. He's a no-good, dirty rotten scoundrel.
ad hominem abusive

2. I don't believe you; you got that information from The Nation and that's just a liberal rag.
genetic fallacy

3. How can you tell me to "just say no," today, Dad, when you said yes in the 60's?
tu quoque

4. Why should I give any weight to your arguments for legal reform? You're a lawyer and probably stand to benefit from such reforms.
ad hominem circumstantial

CUMULATIVE FALLACY QUIZ I

I. DEFINITIONS:

PART A: Name the fallacy that is described.

1. A speaker tries to convince us by making us feel sorry for himself or others.
agumentum ad misericordiam (appeal to pity)

2. An appeal to various bad consequences that will follow if one doesn't accept the speaker's argument, without showing a clear causal link.
argumentum ad baculum (appeal to fear)

3. Implying that two wrongs make a right by discounting someone's argument solely on the basis that they are not entirely consistent.
tu quoque

4. Appealing to the emotions of a crowd or to the common man to make up for a lack of solid evidence or sound reasoning.
argumentum ad populum (mob appeal)

5. Discounting a rival's argument solely on the basis of certain circumstances surrounding them.
ad hominem circumstantial

PART B: Define the following fallacies.

1. SNOB APPEAL: **ANSWERS MAY VARY; EXAMPLE:**
Appealing to a sense of elitism or making someone want to feel like a part of a select group in order to convince them.

2. AD HOMINEM ABUSIVE: **ANSWERS MAY VARY; EXAMPLE:**
Making negative attacks against one's opponent in order to avoid the main issue.

3. GENETIC FALLACY: **ANSWERS MAY VARY; EXAMPLE:**
Rejecting an idea merely because of its origins.

II. EXAMPLES:

Directions: Write both the general category and the specific fallacy committed under each example. *Remember*: Give the reason why you picked the answer that you picked in order to get partial credit.

1. You have no right to speak on the issue of poverty; you've never been poor, so you don't know what it's like.
ad hominem circumstantial

2. It's clear that Al D'Amato's investigation of the president was just a partisan attack. What else would you expect from such a vain and vindictive man. Him losing the election was great for New York.
ad hominem abusive

K

3. Of course those legislators from North Carolina are against this tobacco regulation only because they're in the pockets of the industry. You can't take any of their arguments seriously.
ad hominem circumstance

4. If you don't speak up for the oppressed minorities in this country, by enacting legislation against hate crimes, prejudice and violence will increase.
ad baculum fallacy

5. You really ought to take Jen to the prom, Jon. I know that you're not dating her anymore, but just think of how sad and lonely she'll be all alone at home on the night of her senior prom.
ad misericordiam fallacy

6. I know it was dumb to jump out of a moving car, Nathan, but you did it too.
tu quoque

7. Since the Christian Coalition's opinions derive from religious convictions, their views should have no place in the public square, since we believe in a separation of church and state in this country.
ad hominem circumstantial

8. Please trust that I have the best ideas for furthering the interests of working families in all of my policies, because I feel your pain.
ad misericordiam fallacy

9. Ladies and gentlemen, accepting Jesus into your heart is like buying an eternal life insurance policy to protect you from the fires of Hell. Look, even if you're wrong, and Christianity is false, it won't do you any harm. And if you don't, well, then, you just might be awfully sorry come the judgement day.
ad baculum fallacy

CUMULATIVE FALLACY QUIZ II

I. DEFINITIONS:

PART A: Under each definition, list the fallacy that most closely represents it.

1. An appeal to the mere fact that a belief is widely held to prove its truth.
argumentum ad populum (mob appeal)

2. The classic trick of the demagogue, this fallacy is an appeal to the mystique of the "common man", or the "working man".
argumentum ad populum (mob appeal)

3. This is an appeal to those of "discriminating tastes."
snob appeal

4. This fallacy occurs when the speaker depends on emotional appeals to make his audience feel sorry for himself or others in the place of sound evidence.
argumentum ad misericordiam (appeal to pity)

5. This is an illegitimate appeal to the opinion of an expert. The most common situations in which this occurs are when the expert is not named, is biased or when he is not really an expert in the field in question.
argumentum ad verecumdiam (appeal to illegitimate authority)

6. This is an appeal to the mere age of a belief or practice as evidence that it is correct.
chronological snobbery

PART B: Beside each fallacy name, write the definition of the fallacy.

1. AD HOMINEM ABUSIVE **ANSWERS MAY VARY; EXAMPLE:**
Saying all sorts of mean and nasty things about someone in lieu of a relevant argument.

2. AD HOMINEM CIRCUMSTANTIAL **ANSWERS MAY VARY; EXAMPLE:**
Distracting attention from the main issue by drawing attention to the circumstances surrounding your opponent.

3. TU QUOQUE **ANSWERS MAY VARY; EXAMPLE:**
Saying that one's opponent has no right to argue his point because he has not always been consistent with his own argument.

4. GENETIC FALLACY **ANSWERS MAY VARY; EXAMPLE:**
Saying that the source of an idea automatically discounts it.

K

II. EXAMPLES:

1. Check out the Ford F-150; it's the best selling vehicle in America.
argumentum ad populum (mob appeal)

2. Yuengling Lager: made by the oldest brewery in America.
chronological snobbery

3. Anyone opposing the legislation concerning zero emissions vehicles cannot possibly have the welfare of our environment at heart.
argumentum ad baculum

4. Twin Brooks Winery: no other Lancaster County winery has dedicated itself to producing the classic French varietals with such single-minded devotion. Only the best grapes make it into our bottles.
snob appeal

5. Hi, I'm Tom Hanks. I've got a great idea. Why don't we all just respect each other's differences. Wouldn't that be a great political platform.
argumentum ad verecundiam (appeal to illegitimate authority)

6. People who know cars use Valvoline!
snob appeal

7. Our educational system is in crisis right now and you suggest we engage in risky experiments with untried ideas like vouchers. Surely you don't want our educational system to collapse around our ears and leave us all without enough schools to educate our children!
argumentum ad baculum (appeal to fear)

8. Ladies and gentlemen, those who are opposed to this measure are the lowest kind of base cowards that could possibly be imagined. Do no allow their silly indecisiveness to influence your voting.
ad hominem abusive

9. Back in the days of slavery, they had an old saying. There were those slaves who had the privilege of living in the house and in order to get this privilege, they had to serve the master the way he wanted to be served. Colin Powel is like one of those house slaves serving his master, George Bush, faithfully, but if he steps out of line, he might be sent back into the fields. (Paraphrased from statements by Harry Belefante.)
ad hominem abusive (notice how he is essentially calling Powell a lackey or an "uncle Tom.")

10. How can George Bush have any credibility when speaking of the dangers of alcohol? He admits to having had alcohol problems himself.
tu quoque

III. OPTIONAL SUPPLEMENT ON APPEALS TO AUTHORITY:

Directions: for each of the examples below, name which of the five tests for appeals to authority it fails.

1. "According to sources close to the President, he is prepared to resign if articles of impeachment are passed."
unnamed sources

2. Hi, I'm Dan Marino. If you need a loan, let me tell you, you won't get a better deal than what you'll get from the folks at the Money Store.
authority transference (celebrity endorsement: note that his expertise might carry some weight if he were talking about football, since he's a well-regarded NFL quarterback).

3. Dr. Stone has a PhD in Economics and he says the Dow Jones Industrial is going to drop 600 points next year, so you better cash in your stocks as soon as possible.
limitations of the field

4. There's no such thing as flying squirrels. My big brother said so, so there!
not an authority

5. According to the Rainbow Coalition, we need more money to save our public schools, so it you don't agree that we ought to raise taxes, then you obviously don't care about education.
biased authority (Jackson is a well-known partisan political liberal activist).

6. My dad's a scientist and he says Creationism is bunk, so he must be right.
limitations of the field and/ or bias (There are plenty of brillian, well-educated scientists on both sides of this issue).

Red Herrings Logic Quiz:

I. DEFINITIONS:

1. IRRELEVANT THESIS: **ANSWERS MAY VARY; EXAMPLE:**
An argument that proves the wrong point

2. IRRELEVANT GOALS/ FUNCTIONS: **ANSWERS MAY VARY; EXAMPLE:**
Judging something on the basis of a goal or function that it was never intended to achieve.

3. STRAW MAN: **ANSWERS MAY VARY; EXAMPLE:**
Refuting a distorted portrayal of one's opponent's position.

4. APPEAL TO IGNORANCE: **ANSWERS MAY VARY; EXAMPLE:**
Saying that because something hasn't been disproven, it must be likely.

II. EXAMPLES:

1. Why are you so insistent on asking for proof that there is a ghost haunting the widow Maloney's mansion? You haven't given me any proof that there isn't.
appeal to ignorance

2. I can't support the impeachment of the president. The people supporting it are just a bunch of people obsessed with getting the President on any little thing they can find.
straw man

3. President Reagan: "Don't make age an issue in this campaign. After all, I've never raised the issue of my opponent's youth and inexperience."
irrelevant thesis

4. Don't give me all those old tired lines about being pro life. You're for the death penalty and that's not pro-life.
irrelevant thesis

5. If you cannot absolutely disprove my atheism by giving an airtight argument for the existence of God that I can accept, then the only logical conclusion that can be reached is that we should live our lives as though there is no God.
appeal to ignorance

6. Why would you major in history? You don't want to teach history, so you wouldn't have a very marketable job.
irrelevant goals/ functions

7. Taoism doesn't make any sense. All it is is a bunch of trite obvious sayings said with a certain rhetorical gravity so they impress the gullible into thinking that they are profound.
straw man

8. A Puritan is someone who is terribly afraid that somewhere, somehow, someone might be having some fun.
straw man

CUMULATIVE LOGIC QUIZ III

I. DEFINITIONS:

PART A: This fallacy results from...

1. ... arguing against a caricatured or exaggerated version of an opponent's position.
straw man

2. ...arguing that because someone cannot disprove our position that it must be right.
appeal to ignorance

3. ...calling our opponent all sorts of nasty names rather than challenging his argument.
ad hominem abusive

4. ...proving a different point than the one that is relevant to the issue at hand.
irrelevant thesis

5. ...accepting an illegitimate appeal to the authority of an expert.
appeal to illegitimate authority

6. ...arguing that a practice is not the right one because it doesn't fulfill a purpose for which it was never intended.
irrelevant goals/ functions

PART B: Give the definition for each fallacy below.

1. AD HOMINEM CIRCUMSTANTIAL: **ANSWERS MAY VARY; EXAMPLE:**
Rejecting a speaker's argument solely because of some circumstances surrounding him, frequently with an implication that his argument is solely based on self-interest.

2. MOB APPEAL: **ANSWERS MAY VARY; EXAMPLE:**
Appealing to the popularity of a belief or the emotions of a crowd.

3. SNOB APPEAL: **ANSWERS MAY VARY; EXAMPLE:**
making the listener want to be part of an elite.

4. CHRONOLOGICAL SNOBBERY: **ANSWERS MAY VARY; EXAMPLE:**
Accepting or rejecting and idea solely based on it age.

5. GENETIC FALLACY: **ANSWERS MAY VARY; EXAMPLE:**
Rejecting a belief solely based on its origins.

6. TU QUOQUE **ANSWERS MAY VARY; EXAMPLE:**
Implying that someone has no right to talk because they did it too.

K

II. EXAMPLES:

1. How can the prosecution seriously suggest that my client committed this brutal crime? He's a fine, upstanding pillar of this community and a dedicated family man loved by all.
appeal to pity. (This is sort of a reverse "ad hominem circumstantial," since his circumstances are being used to ask you to believe him rather than disbelieve him).

2. The only reason why you oppose this badly-needed reform measure for reporting corporate income is because you're an accountant and you have much to gain by the current system.
ad hominem circumstantial (Notice the self-interest angle on this one).

3. Feminists like her only believe in women's lib because they hate men.
ad hominem abusive (or circumstantial if she really does hate men).

4. Christmas is a pagan, Roman, commercialized holiday. Christians shouldn't celebrate it.
genetic fallacy

5. Don't major in philosophy. My father used to say that when you're sick, you go to a doctor, when you're in trouble you need a lawyer, but every man has his own philosophy!
irrelevant goals/ functions

6. Don't tell me that I can't prove that the president has been involved in multiple murder conspiracies. You can't prove that he isn't.
appeal to ignorance

7. There's nothing wrong with polygamy. After all, it was practiced in even the oldest civilizations of which we have records.
chronological snobbery

LOGIC QUARTERFINAL I
(Unit 1)

I. DEFINITIONS:

1. AD HOMINEM ABUSIVE: **ANSWERS MAY VARY; EXAMPLE:**
Using insults against a rival to distract the audience.

2. AD HOMINEM CIRCUMSTANTIAL: **ANSWERS MAY VARY; EXAMPLE:**
Using the circumstances of a rival to distract the audience.

3. TU QUOQUE: **ANSWERS MAY VARY; EXAMPLE:**
Insisting that one's rival has no room to criticize something because they've done it before.

4. GENETIC FALLACY: **ANSWERS MAY VARY; EXAMPLE:**
Using the origins of an idea to discount it.

5. APPEAL TO FEAR: **ANSWERS MAY VARY; EXAMPLE:**
Trying to convince someone by playing on their fears.

6. APPEAL TO PITY: **ANSWERS MAY VARY; EXAMPLE:**
Trying to convince someone by playing on their sense of pity.

7. MOB APPEAL: **ANSWERS MAY VARY; EXAMPLE:**
Trying to convince someone by playing on their desire to be part of the group.

8. APPEAL TO ILLEGITIMATE AUTHORITY: **ANSWERS MAY VARY; EXAMPLE:**
Trying to convince someone by playing on their respect for an expert, authority or a famous person.

9. SNOB APPEAL: **ANSWERS MAY VARY; EXAMPLE:**
Trying to persuade someone by playing on their desire to be part of an elite.

10. CHRONOLOGICAL SNOBBERY: **ANSWERS MAY VARY; EXAMPLE:**
Appealing to the age of something to get others to accept or reject it.

11. APPEAL TO IGNORANCE: **ANSWERS MAY VARY; EXAMPLE:**
Abusing the burden of proof by arguing that if something hasn't been disproven, it must be likely.

12. IRRELEVANT THESIS: **ANSWERS MAY VARY; EXAMPLE:**
Making the case for the wrong point.

13. IRRELEVANT GOALS AND FUNCTIONS: **ANSWERS MAY VARY; EXAMPLE:**
Judging something according to goals that are irrelevant or unrealistic.

14. STRAW MAN: **ANSWERS MAY VARY; EXAMPLE:**
Distorting one's opponent's position.

II. EXAMPLES:

A. PERSONAL ATTACKS/ AD FONTEM ARGUMENTS

1. I can't believe that you would give his ideas any credence. He's nothing but a long-haired, maggot-infested, dope-smoking, FM type.
ad hominem abusive

2. You only favor a capital gains tax cut because you own lots of stock and stand to benefit.
ad hominem circumstantial

3. The only reason that you believe in God is because you have felt a need for a father figure and have built a wish projection onto reality for a paternal God.
genetic fallacy or ad hominem circumstantial (The latter is a possibility because the argument sounds like it's addressed to one individual person; the former is better, because the argument is really about the origins of the belief, not the situation of the believer).

4. Why did you put my name on the board for talking? Everyone else was talking too.
tu quoque

B. EMOTIONAL APPEALS

1. Don't vote for these country-club, blue-blooded Republicans. Vote for John Jackson, champion of the American working man.
argumentum ad populum (mob appeal)

2. Those Gingrich Republicans are the ones you should beware of. They're coming for our children, they're coming for the elderly...
argumentum ad baculum (appeal to fear; this is a better answer here than appeal to pity because of the way lends a sense of impending doom more so than emphasizes the wretchedness of the potential victims.)

3. Esteemed members of Congress, have pity on the poor American taxpayer, taxed more than at any other time in history. Please, gentlemen, lighten his load by accepting this tax cut proposal.
argumentum ad misericordiam (appeal to pity)

4. Cars do so run on water! My big brother told me so, so there!
appeal to illegitimate authority

5. Smoke Camel Regulars: they're the real man's cigarette.
snob appeal (appeals to an elite group, the group of "real men").

6. Polygamy must be OK, since it goes back as far back as recorded history.
chronological snobbery

7. Buy a Ford F-150, the best-selling vehicle in America!
argumentum ad populum (mob appeal)

C. RED HERRINGS

1. I don't see why we're spending so much on the so-called "war on drugs". Alcohol is far more frequently abused and it's still legal.
irrelevant goals/ functions

2. Our political opponents have challenged us to give them evidence that there really is a "health-care crisis." Well I ask them to give us some evidence that there isn't.
appeal to ignorance

3. Those Christian Right activists are just a bunch of homophobes who encourage violence against homosexuals.
straw man

4. Let's get serious here, gentlemen; giving the American people a tax cut is not going to solve all of their financial problems.
irrelevant goals/ functions

CUMULATIVE FALLACY QUIZ IV

I. DEFINITIONS:
PART A: *This fallacy is committed when...*

1. ...the speaker makes the assumption that the parts will have the same properties as a collective whole.
division

2. ...the speaker is either just restating the conclusion in other words or uses a justification that is more controversial than the original conclusion.
begging the question

3. ...the speaker assumes that a collective whole will have the properties of the sum of its parts.
composition

4. ...the speaker assumes that something is the right thing simply because it is the way that things happen to be.
is-ought fallacy

5. ...the speaker assumes that the best solution to a problem is necessarily a compromise between extremes.
fallacy of moderation

6. ...the speaker assumes that only two possibilities exist, when in fact there may be others.
bifurcation/ false dilemma

PART B: Give the definition for the fallacy named.

1. AD HOMINEM ABUSIVE **ANSWERS MAY VARY; EXAMPLE:**
Using negative personal attacks on one's opponent to distract from the main issue

2. GENETIC FALLACY **ANSWERS MAY VARY; EXAMPLE:**
Using the origin of an idea or belief to discredit it.

3. APPEAL TO ILLEGITIMATE AUTHORITY **ANSWERS MAY VARY; EXAMPLE:**
Using an inappropriate appeal to someone's expertise or fame to support an argument.

4. TU QUOQUE **ANSWERS MAY VARY; EXAMPLE:**
Using an opponent's past inconsistency to discount his current argument

5. STRAW MAN **ANSWERS MAY VARY; EXAMPLE:**
Using a distorted version of an opponent's position to discredit him.

6. IRRELEVANT GOALS/ FUNCITONS **ANSWERS MAY VARY; EXAMPLE:**
Using an irrelevant or unrealistic goal or function to discredit an idea or practice.

7. IRRELEVANT THESIS **ANSWERS MAY VARY; EXAMPLE:**
Using an argument making the wrong point to distract the argument from the real point.

8. CHRONOLOGICAL SNOBBERY **ANSWERS MAY VARY; EXAMPLE:**
Using the age of something as the sole reason why it should be accepted or rejected.

Quiz Key } *The Art of Argument*

II. EXAMPLES:

1. Look, if those Bosnian Serbs and Muslims can't live together, why don't we just split the land in half and give half to each of them?
fallacy of moderation

2. No Christian can, in good conscience, serve in the military. One can either be a man of peace or a man of war and the Christian's Lord is the Prince of Peace.
bifurcation/ false dilemma

3. Look: I'm a soldier because that is what I am. That is what I've always been and it's all that I know.
is-ought fallacy

4. "These three musketeers are valiant men, and consummate swordsmen. If I had an army of such men, we would be unstoppable!"
fallacy of composition

5.   **Mr. Engleton:** Dickens' works are much better literature than those of Tolkien.
       Johnny: How does one know which works are great literature?
       Mr. Engleton: They are the ones recommended by the well-informed.
       Johnny: How does one get to be well-informed?
       Mr. Engleton: Why, by reading great works of literature like Dickens, of course.
begging the question

6. The men who wrote this program had worked for Microsoft, the most powerful, successful, hard-driving company in the software industry. They must have been great programmers themselves.
fallacy of division (notice how this argument implies something about the individuals based on a knowledge of the whole).

Fallacies of Induction Quiz

I. DEFINITIONS:

PART A: Give the fallacy of induction that best fits the following description.

1. Basing an argument on a comparison of two examples that don't have enough similarity.
false analogy

2. Creating a generalization on the basis of too few examples.
hasty generalization

3. Basing an argument on a weak causal connection.
false cause

4. Extending a generalization to exceptional cases.
sweeping generalization

5. The misuse of statistics
fake precision

PART B: Give the definition for the fallacy named below:

1. FALLACY OF COMPOSITION **ANSWERS MAY VARY; EXAMPLE:**
Assuming that the whole will have the same properties as the parts.

2. FALLACY OF MODERATION **ANSWERS MAY VARY; EXAMPLE:**
Assuming that the answer is always in a compromise between extremes.

3. IS-OUGHT FALLACY **ANSWERS MAY VARY; EXAMPLE:**
Assuming that just because something is a certain way that it ought to be.

4. BIFURCATION **ANSWERS MAY VARY; EXAMPLE:**
Assuming that there are only two options when there may be more.

5. BEGGING THE QUESTION **ANSWERS MAY VARY; EXAMPLE:**
An argument that "begs more questions" than it answers.

6. FALLACY OF DIVISION **ANSWERS MAY VARY; EXAMPLE:**
Assuming that the parts will have the same characteristics as a collective whole.

7. TU QUOQUE **ANSWERS MAY VARY; EXAMPLE:**
Arguing that someone's argument should be discounted because they have not always been consistent with it.

8. STRAW MAN **ANSWERS MAY VARY; EXAMPLE:**
Using a distorted picture of an opponent's position to discredit them.

9. CHRONOLOGICAL SNOBBERY **ANSWERS MAY VARY; EXAMPLE:**
Using the age of an idea or practice to prove or disprove it.

II. EXAMPLES: (Careful: there's one Fallacy of Presupposition buried in here to keep

you on your toes)!

1. It's no wonder that violent crime has increased lately, what with all those violent Hollywood movies they make lately!
false cause (causal oversimplifcation)

2. We shouldn't let kids watch those violent Hollywood movies because it just isn't right for them to see such images of brutality and hurtfulness.
begging the question

3. After all, people who watch violent movies have 4 times as many violent thoughts as those who do not.
fake precision

4. You know that guy Tommy watches violent movies all the time and he gets into fights all the time, so it's obvious that violent movies cause people to be violent.
hasty generalization OR false cause

5. Since people who watch violent movies are four times as likely to commit violent crimes, Jon-boy is more likely to commit one if he watches such movies. (Assume that these numbers are based on a legitimate study).
sweeping generalization

6. Since that guy Tommy gets into fights and he watches violent movies, Johnny will do just the same if he watches violent movies.
false analogy

7. OK, so you've finally conceded that Stallone movies are too violent. Three Stooges movies are out too, because of all the hitting and striking that goes on in those violent flicks.
false analogy

CUMULATIVE FALLACY QUIZ V

I. DEFINITIONS:

1. BEGGING THE QUESTION: **ANSWERS MAY VARY; EXAMPLE:**
An argument that is either circular or relies on highly controversial premises.

2. BIFURCATION/FALSE DILEMMA: **ANSWERS MAY VARY; EXAMPLE:**
An argument that assumes only two alternatives are possible when there may very well be others.

3. FALLACY OF MODERATION: **ANSWERS MAY VARY; EXAMPLE:**
Assuming that compromise is always good for its own sake.

4. FALLACY OF COMPOSITION: **ANSWERS MAY VARY; EXAMPLE:**
Assuming that the whole will have the same characteristics as the parts.

5. FALLACY OF DIVISION: **ANSWERS MAY VARY; EXAMPLE:**
Assuming that the parts will have the same characteristics as the whole.

6. IS-OUGHT FALLACY: **ANSWERS MAY VARY; EXAMPLE:**
Assuming that just because something is a certain way that it ought to be that way.

7. SWEEPING GENERALIZATION (ACCIDENT): **ANSWERS MAY VARY; EXAMPLE:**
Extending a generalization further than it ought to be extended.

8. HASTY GENERALIZATION (CONVERSE ACCIDENT): **ANSWERS MAY VARY; EXAMPLE:**
Making a generalization too quickly.

9. FALSE ANALOGY: **ANSWERS MAY VARY; EXAMPLE:**
Making an argument based on an analogy between two things that just aren't similar enough.

10. FALSE CAUSE: **ANSWERS MAY VARY; EXAMPLE:**
Basing an argument on a weak causal connection.

11. FAKE PRECISION: **ANSWERS MAY VARY; EXAMPLE:**
The misuse of statistics in an argument.

II. EXAMPLES:

PART A: Select from the following three possibilities: *False Analogy, Hasty Generalization, Sweeping Generalization*

1. People who make bad grades usually do so because they do not study. Since Jack is making bad grades, it's obvious that he doesn't study.
sweeping generalization

2. John admits that his problems in school are a result of a lack of effort. Jack is struggling, too, so that must be his problem, too.
false analogy

3. John and Susie just don't try very hard at school. Kids these days are just so lazy.
hasty generalization

PART B: Select from the following possibilities: ***False Cause, Fake Precision, Composition and Division.***

1. Dennis Rodman is a great basketball player. When they add him to Shaquille O'Neal and Kobe Bryant, they are sure to have a great team.
fallacy of composition

2. Any law against partial birth abortion will be very unpopular. After all, a recent study by the People for the American Way showed that 82% of people believe in reproductive rights for women.
fake precision (The study, even if accepted at face value, makes no mention of partial-birth abortion and is thus no evidence of the claim made; these statistics are thus being misused.)

3. Studies show that most elementary school teachers are parents. It must be because working with children stimulates an interest in parenthood.
false cause (probably neglect of a common cause; people who love children are both more likely to have them and to go into elementary education).

4. John Elway needs to be elected MVP of the NFL. After all, his team is the best team in the league right now.
fallacy of division

PART C: Select from the following possibilities: ***Begging the Question, Is-ought, Bifurcation, Moderation***

1. Of course abortion is OK. It's a legal activity, isn't it?
is-ought (It's legal... but ought it to be?).

2. The solution to the Kosovo crisis is obvious: why don't the Serbs just give Kosovo the same status as Montinegro, as a separate republic within Yugoslavia. Then the Serbs and Albanians could just compromise and get along.
fallacy of moderation

3. Since you started 8 months ago, you have consistently had the lowest sales in the Department. If you haven't figured out what it is that your problem is, you obviously don't understand the business. If you have figured it out and haven't corrected it, you don't learn from your mistakes. Either way, you are a proven failure as an employee and we can't afford to keep such people on the payroll.
bifurcation (Surely there are other possibilities).

4. We need a Women's History month because women need a special time to celebrate their own achievements.
begging the question (But why do we need such a special time? The argument is really circular).

PART D: Select from the following possibilities: *Hasty Generalization, Sweeping Generalization, Composition and Division.*

1. That blimp is a lighter than air vehicle. That must mean that everything on it is lighter than air.
division

2. People who live on Lookout Mountain are mostly pretty wealthy. Your friend Greg lives on Lookout Mountain, so he must be loaded.
sweeping generalization

3. Jon, Mike and I are not as athletic as those guys. There's no way we could put together a team that could beat them.
composition

4. My Uncle Harry is a crazy driver. It must be a quality common to all people from Queens.
hasty generalization

CUMULATIVE FALLACY QUIZ VI

I. DEFINITIONS:

1. Ambiguity that is created by the fact that a word has more than one meaning is...
equivocation

2. Confusion that is created by misplaced stress on one particular word or syllable is...
accent

3. Confusion caused by treating a purely semantic distinction as if it were a real distinction.
distinction without a difference

II. EXAMPLES:

1. He said that this dress looks good on me. I can't believe he would imply that the other doesn't.
accent

2. Mr. Jones must be a very responsible person. If anything goes wrong at Lewis Academy, he is held responsible.
equivocation (on "responsible")

3. Jack isn't an angry person. He just flies into a rage and hurts people every once in a while.
distinction without a difference

III. REVIEW DEFINITIONS:

1. BEGGING THE QUESTION: **ANSWERS MAY VARY; EXAMPLE:**
An argument that either assumes itself or assumes something that is at least as doubtful as the conclusion itself.

2. BIFURCATION/FALSE DILEMMA: **ANSWERS MAY VARY; EXAMPLE:**
Unjustifiably assuming that there are only two possibilities.

3. FALLACY OF MODERATION: **ANSWERS MAY VARY; EXAMPLE:**
Assuming that compromise is always the right choice.

4. FALLACY OF COMPOSITION: **ANSWERS MAY VARY; EXAMPLE:**
Assuming that the whole will have the same characteristics as the parts.

5. FALLACY OF DIVISION: **ANSWERS MAY VARY; EXAMPLE:**
Assuming that the parts will have the same characteristics as the whole.

6. IS-OUGHT FALLACY: **ANSWERS MAY VARY; EXAMPLE:**
Assuming that something ought to be a certain way, just because it is that way.

7. SWEEPING GENERALIZATION (ACCIDENT): **ANSWERS MAY VARY; EXAMPLE:**
Assuming that something that is generally true must always be true.
8. HASTY GENERALIZATION (CONVERSE ACCIDENT): **ANSWERS MAY VARY; EXAMPLE:**

K

Assuming that something that is only observed a few times must be generallys true.

9. FALSE ANALOGY: **ANSWERS MAY VARY; EXAMPLE:**
An argument based on a comparison of two things that aren't enough alike.

10. FALSE CAUSE: **ANSWERS MAY VARY; EXAMPLE:**
Basing an argument on an insufficiently established causal connection.

11. FAKE PRECISION: **ANSWERS MAY VARY; EXAMPLE:**
The inappropriate use of statistics.

LOGIC QUARTERFINAL II
(Unit II)

I. DEFINITIONS: Write out the definitions for the following fallacies.

1. EQUIVOCATION: **ANSWERS MAY VARY; EXAMPLE:**
An argument that turns on a word that changes in meaning.

2. ACCENT: **ANSWERS MAY VARY; EXAMPLE:**
An argument that turns on the emphasis placed on one word or in which a speaker is taken out of context.

3. DISTINCTION WITHOUT A DIFFERENCE: **ANSWERS MAY VARY; EXAMPLE:**
Confusing a semantic distinction with a real one.

II. DEFINITIONS: Name which fallacy goes with the following definitions

1. Making a generalization based on too few examples is...
hasty generalization

2. Building an argument based on a comparison of two things that ought not be compared is...
false analogy

3. Applying a generalization to exceptional circumstances that it ought not apply to is...
sweeping generalization

4. Drawing conclusions about a collective whole based on the characteristics of the parts is...
composition

5. Drawing conclusions about the parts of a collective whole based on the characteristics of the whole is...
division

6. Making an argument that is either circular or rests on premises that are more controversial than the conclusions is...
begging the question

7. Misusing statistics is...
fake precision

8. Building an argument on a weak causal connection is...
false cause

9. Assuming that the truth is always a middle ground between extremes is...
fallacy of moderation

10. Building an argument on a false dilemma is...
bifurcation

11. Assuming that something is right simply because it happens to be that way is...
is-ought fallacy

III. EXAMPLES: Choose from the following: *hasty generalization, sweeping generalization and false analogy*

1. English majors are legendary for not being good at math. Gordon was an English major, so he's not going to do well in my college Algebra class.
sweeping generalizations

2. Scott wasn't very good at math. English majors must not be very talented at it.
hasty generalization

3. Since Scott, an English major, did poorly at math, it's obvious that Gordon, an English major as well, will have trouble.
false analogy

IV EXAMPLES: Choose from the following: ***Begging the Question, Equivocation, Distinction Without a Difference, Accent and Bifurcation.***

1. There are laws of nature. Laws imply a lawgiver. Therefore, there must be a Cosmic lawgiver.
eqivocation (There are different kinds of laws; are Cosmic laws the same type as the ones that imply a law-giver).

2. There are two types of people in the world: those who own Mercedes-Benz automobiles and those who wish they did.
bifurcation

3. There is no such thing as knowledge which cannot be put into practice, for such knowledge is no knowledge at all. (Confucius)
begging the question

4. Only Hollywood could produce a film like this.
accent

5. I'm not a poor student. I just don't study very hard.
distinction without a difference

V. EXAMPLES: Choose from the following: ***Hasty Generalization, Sweeping Generalization, Composition and Division.***

1. Cars put out less pollution than buses. Therefore, an increase in emphasis on busing will also increase pollution levels.
composition

2. Weiss Markets has a lower price on milk and eggs than Giant. I'll save money if I shop there.
hasty generalization

3. Studies show that taking regular doses of Vitamin C can prevent sickness. If I take these Vitamin pills, I should stay healthy.
sweeping generalization

4. The Roman legions dominated the battlefield for 400 years. The legionaries must have been the best warriors of their time.
division

VI EXAMPLES: Choose from the following: *False Cause, Fake Precision, Fallacy of Moderation and Is-ought Fallacy.*

1. You said that one must come to class, participate in discussion and read the material in order to do well in the class. I did all of these things, and yet I only got a C. Why?
false cause (confusing a necessary and a sufficient condition)

2. "Mr. and Mrs. Cain; I know that you're going through a rough patch in your relationship. Let's just begin by admitting that you are both probably in the wrong on many things."
moderation

3. Public Affairs is not really the most important thing for a president to spend his time on. The public doesn't seem to care that much and the administration treats it as an afterthought.
is-ought

4. When the average salary of all men and all women is factored, the women's average is only $.74 to every dollar that men earn.
fake precision (These studies don't usually compare apples and apples.)

Notes